BOOKS BY DENISE LOW

<u>Poetry</u>
Thailand Journal: Poems
New & Selected Poems 1980-1999
Tulip Elegies: An Alchemy of Writing
Vanishing Point (limited edition)
Selective Amnesia (Stiletto I)
Starwater
Learning the Language of Rivers (*Midwest Quarterly*)
Spring Geese and Other Poems
Quilting (fine press edition)
Dragon Kite (*Mid-America Trio*)

<u>Prose</u>
*Natural Theologies: Essays about Literature of the New
     Middle West*
To the Stars: Kansas Poets of the Ad Astra Project
3 Voices: Seasons, Shrines, &Portraits, (images & text)
*From Kansas to Harlem: Midwestern Heritage of Langston
     Hughes*
Words of a Prairie Alchemist: Essays
Langston Hughes in Lawrence, with T.F. Weso
Touching the Sky

<u>Edited</u>
Kansas Poems of William Stafford
Wakarusa Wetlands in Word and Image
Teaching Leslie Marmon Silko's Ceremony, with Peter G. Beidler
The Good Earth: Three Poets of the Prairie
Confluence: Contemporary Kansas Poetry
30 Kansas Poets

GHOST STORIES OF THE NEW WEST:

From Einstein's Brain to Geronimo's Boots

by

DENISE LOW

WOODLEY MEMORIAL PRESS
WASHBURN UNIVERSITY

ISBN 978-0-9817334-9-4
Library of Congress Control Number: 2010931733
Printed by Lightning Source

Editing by Kevin Rabas of Woodley Memorial Press
Cover art by Thomas Pecore Weso
Cover design by Blue Heron, Lawrence, Kansas

WOODLEY MEMORIAL PRESS/ ENGLISH DEPARTMENT
WASHBURN UNIVERSITY/ TOPEKA, KANSAS 66621

http://www.washburn.edu/reference/woodley-press

I appreciate the kindly support of:

My husband, the incomparable Thomas Pecore Weso
Book mentor and editor Kevin Rabas, a fine poet and friend
Woodley Press, especially Karen Barron, Dennis Etzel, Larry McGurn, and
    founder Bob Lawson
Family: David & Ginny Dotson, Jane & Mark Ciabattari, David Low &
    Allison Thomas, Daniel Low & Celine Carbullido, Pemecewan
    Wesosa Fleuker & Josh Meisel, Curtis Monroe Fleuker, Bob &
    Theress Bruner, Robin Bruner, Barbara & Jerry Johnson, Wesos and
    Walkers in Menominee County, Diane & Don Low
Many friends, including: Caryn Mirriam-Goldberg (2009-2011 Kansas
    Poet Laureate), Judith Roitman & Stanley Lombardo, Jennie James,
    Teddi & Bill James and Leatha Pearl, Michael & Pamela Tambornino,
    Kathryn Kysar & Riding Shotgun sisters, Diane Willie, Bob & Kathy
    Day, Fred Whitehead, Mohamed El-Hodiri, Luci Tapahonso &
    Robert Martin, and Jonathan Holden, first poet laureate of Kansas
Three Voices collaborator and friend Paul Hotvedt
Colleagues on the Associated Writing Programs board & staff
Imagination & Place colleagues, the Tellers Group, the PTs Coffee Group,
    Lawrence Women's Writers Group, Lawrence Arts Center, The
    Writers Place of Kansas City, and Big Tent curators
Former Governor Kathleen Sebelius, who initiated the Kansas poet
    laureate position
The Kansas Arts Commission folks, including Llewellyn Crain, Christine
    Bial, and Margaret Morris

My thanks to these publications and their editors where poems, sometimes in earlier version, first appeared:

Caprice: "Underground Wonder Bar, Chicago," "Trumpeter Swan"
Chariton Review: "Double-Crested Cormorants," "Summer Warbler"
Chiron Review: "Carrie A. Nation," "Custer's Sleigh," "Haunted Road"
Coal City Review: "A Ghost at Watertower Park," "Wilson's Snipe"
Connecticut Review: "Funeral Fire"
Connotation Press, Congeries (Ed. John Hoppenthaler): "A Lenape Indian Grandfather's Biography," "Photograph of The Kansas Anti-Horse Thief Association Annual Convention," "Willows"
Dust & Fire: Women's Stories: "Pontiac Hall Ghost"
Evensong (Huron: Bottom Dog, 2006. Eds. Gerry LaFemina and Chad Prevost): "Columbarium Garden," "Flint Hills Twilight," "Menominee Rez"
Flint Hills Review: "Scenes after the Death of William Burroughs"
I-70 Review: "Eureka Springs Winter," "Geronimo's Boots Leave Town," "Exhibition Box of Meadowlarks," "Celebrity Bingo"
In the Black/In the Red: Poems of Profit & Loss: "My Grandfather Raises Rabbits" (Los Angeles: Helicon 9 Editions, 2010. Eds. Phil Miller and Gloria Vando)
Kansas City Star: "Deer Season," "Tornado Angels," "I Miss You Sonny Kenner," "Osage Beach, Lake of the Ozarks," "Flint Hills National Grasslands," "Mallard"
Kansas City Voices: "A Moundbuilder's Geography"
Mikrokosmos: "Cloud Break"
New Mexico Poetry Review: "Cherokee Wedding Poem"
Poems of the Kansas Plains (Manhattan: Kansas State University, 2006. Ed. Priscilla McKinney): "Trailhead," "Red-Tail Hawk," "Turkey Buzzards, Meade County"
The Poets Guide to the Birds (Tallahassee: Anhinga, 2008. Eds. Judith Kitchen & Ted Kooser): "Sparrow"
Seveneightfive Collection (Topeka: Seveneightfive, 2008. Ed. Matt Porubsky): "Taxidermy"
Summerset Review: "Skulk of Foxes," "Conception," "Photography"
Three Voices (Lawrence: Blue Heron, 2008): "Portraiture"
Times of Sorrow (Omaha: The Backwaters Press, 2002. Eds. Marjorie Saiser, Greg Kosmicki and Lisa Sandlin): "Feathers"
Yellow Medicine Review: "Delaware Guardian Doll," "Cloud Break," "Allow Us In," "Gather and Spread," "For the Maiden Aunts and Bachelor Uncles," "Where My Father Went" (Ed. Ralph Salisbury)

Dedicated to Elders of the past

and to

Curtis Monroe (Keso') Fleuker

the future

Contents

I.

For the Maiden Aunts and Bachelor Uncles

For an uncle called Big Miller
killed by Lenape Indians in Ohio.
For Lenape uncles killed by Big Miller.

For Cherokee aunts killed by Jackson's soldiers.
For soldiers drowned by Water Monsters—
the antlered giant fish in deep rivers.

For the cowboy Edwin who died of typhoid.
He lost his chance to gamble, brawl, sin,
and be redeemed.

For the nameless toddler great-uncle
who tipped the boiling coffee pot
and scalded himself to death.

For Great-Aunt Annie who passed
amid a great rush of breath
taking also her sister's certain faith.

For those dead from snakebite, pox,
frostbite, horse kick, stampede, cholera
gunshot, grass fire, and bad water.

For their sunken burials on grassy hillsides.
Dawn sunlight erases chiseled names
and embellishments of white-marble roses.

The Kansas Anti-Horse Thief Association Annual Convention Photograph

I search the crowd of men for faces
I might know, Great-Uncle Ed who was
a drover and gunfighter, not the Quaker Isaiah.
Among the hatless, black-suited men might be
the Delaware grandfathers—former Indian scouts
who fought Spanish, Pawnees, Ruffians and now
horse thieves and rustlers. It is 1913
on this page, and a "vigilance committee"
meets annually, years after the Civil War,
on this borderland of the Chisholm Trail.

My father was born into this town. I remember
his violence-laced language, with vignettes
of lawless alleys, broken arms, and the phrase
"He'd as soon kill you as look at you."
I remember playing mumblety-peg, a game
where we took turns throwing knives as close
to feet as we could without drawing blood.
We prepared for marauders who might engage
us in hand-to-hand combat as others stole horses,
burned buildings, and would not leave until
our brothers and uncles met at Sixth and Main,
posed, and for all time, stood in force.

And you, my reader, might find yourself within
this framed frame, my wording of an image
viewed a century later, and you,
unexpectedly, now stand among that throng
on a windless moment, mild October,
when several hundred warriors gather.
You too might remember outlaws
who shot your grandpa on the Santa Fe train
or the games you played when a child,
ones with dunking, thumping, stoning, shooting—
everything that prepared you for this place.

A Skulk of Foxes

Like the *cherm* or charm of finches, so the skulk of foxes
confounds the twilight. Step-sidling, their auburn pelts shift
into shadows. Cat-like, they stalk mice. Shanks turn black.
Slit eyes catch last yellow sunlight and hold it steady.
They den down the block, under the neighbor's tool shed.

Tomorrow they might turn into fancy stoles or tricksters.
They might turn into ragged coyotes and grin at gardeners.
They could be a skulk of thieves, crouched. Or malingerers.
Under mulberry shrubs they sense human presence. Pause.
Flicker in peripheral vision, softly scatter. But never vacate.

Funeral Fire

For Buddy Weso
"O day and night, but this is wondrous strange!" *Hamlet*

My grandmother said we travel to stars
when we die. This dawn a bonfire hisses
blue flames against banked snow
guiding Uncle's journey from life
into uncertain sky. Clouds obscure
heaven's embers. Around us pines
collect tears from the driving wind.

Across the Wolf River a faint cry
and someone says "*kene*" just as softly
so I barely pick out both the bird's sound
and the spoken Algonquin word
from the burning, breaking splinters
and explosion of popping orange sparks—
familiar fireplace sounds I recognize—

but just as quickly I doubt soft voices
until again, in full daylight, the sound "*kene*."

Kene: Eagle (Menominee)

Ghosts on the Santa Fe Trail

1.
My husband sets our suitcases by the closet. When he
stands up, he sees a ghost, an old woman in a rocking chair.
We are in a Victorian-era hotel on the Santa Fe Trail, and
such sightings are not unusual. I do not see her, but that
side of the room seems occupied. As soon as he tells me
about the ghost, I discern a woman in a long gingham dress,
small-boned and old. Her pale hair, once blonde, is pulled
into a bun. She takes form as completely as though she
were real. Oddly, I realize she is not much older than I am.
In some future, I might walk across the room and find
myself in her world, myself a ghost-person. My life, too,
may reduce to one emblematic posture.

2.
I look out her window. I wonder why she does not peruse
downtown or the nearby Neosho River, where children fish.
Then I notice the overgrown oxbow lake under our window
and realize the river used to flow here. She is looking at the
old riverbed as it was a century ago, not what we see—
unmown reeds and ancient cottonwood trees.

   She stares at a spot that used to be downriver, perhaps
to see if a lover will return. I remember a story about a
Native woman whose French husband went to St. Louis and
never returned. Every morning the bereaved woman
looked for his boat. He may have stayed with another wife
in St. Louis or perhaps he died, but the broken-hearted
woman never remarried. I wonder now if this ghost-woman
is trapped in the same tragedy.

4.
 As I fall asleep, I think of how a life story reduces to a
simple plot line, one of the dozen or so narrative variations
on the human condition: "Boy meets girl," "Hero slays
monster," and "Ghost haunts tragic site." I wonder if this
shadow woman is awaiting a lover, maybe Wild Bill Hickok

or Buffalo Bill Cody. In this town, historic figures of the Old West are not forgotten, and they, too, are ghosts in memories of the living.

5.
Council Grove is a likely site for ghosts. In the 1600s, Spanish and Comanches oversaw a slave trade as well as commerce in furs and other goods. A 1776 cannon was found inexplicably buried in Neosho River mud. In 1821 the first trade caravan left Kansas City to travel this route through Indian Territory to Santa Fe. In 1825, Great and Little Osage leaders signed a right-of-way treaty for the trail, under Council Oak. The last Cheyenne raid on the town was in the 1870s. The old woman ghost may have been a witness.

6.
Much of the old days remain. Old saloons, an Indian mission, a jail, boarding houses, and a meeting house still stand. The town bank is the Farmers and Drovers Bank, and drovers continue to wear chaps, spurs, and cowboy hats. They could be mistaken for apparitions until they climb into oversized pickup trucks.

7.
An old tavern that once housed soldiers now serves as a restaurant. The kitchen staff makes its own pickled beets and water melon rind. The best meals are slabs of prime beef from a local ranch.

George Armstrong Custer ate here, his last sojourn in any town. I wonder where he sat, and if the winds blew hard that last night. Kit Carson, Bill Hickok, and other celebrities of the old West also dined and drank here, and then passed into myth.

The basement bar is the eeriest part of the building. Limestone walls are the original foundation, set in 1857. We visit this bar and drink in the oldest tavern west of the Mississippi. Dark whiskey tastes strong in glass tumblers .

8.
I remember my Grandfather Dotson and his frontier stories.
As a young man, he jogged long distances because the train
came through only once a day. Survival from one laboring
day to the next was a struggle. When he prayed over a meal,
I felt his words came from faith born from hard experience,
not quiet Bible readings in the parlor.

My grandfather often sat and drank coffee with other old
men at places like the Council Grove tavern. He enjoyed
camaraderie of the men's groups who gather at feed stores,
cafés and saloons. They are the Greek chorus of Western
tragedies. They remember fights and weddings and days
when presidents visited on trains. They maintain the roster
of genealogies, in repeating cycles.

9.
Bar fights were real, but miraculous recoveries were not.
One tough cowboy who was kicked in the groin never was
able to have children. He remained bitter the rest of his life.
Other stories are also tragic and cautionary. A teenage
couple married and had a child right away. They lived in a
remote valley, just getting by. That winter, snowed into
their house, they had little food, and the woman lost her
milk. The baby gradually weakened and died.

Most of the stories are about specific places. Kit Carson
engraved Council Grove's name on cowhide and nailed it to
a tree. In the 1870s, the mission teacher could not keep
Kaw Indian students in class. Their parents used the stuffy
stone houses as barns. The old schoolhouse still stands,
refitted as a museum.

10.
I sit by the window and read. A local history book recounts
how one year a hermit-priest stayed in the small cave west
of town. The man, Matteo Boccalini, chiseled religious
graffiti. His only possession was a mandolin. He must have
strummed music to mix with the evening breezes. After
winter, he wandered down the Santa Fe Trail to New

Mexico. A few years later traders said the priest was killed in a Sangre de Christo cave.

I put down the book and look through the window. A distant line of trees shows where the Neosho River continues to flow. Light streams into the room. Ghosts hold their silence.

11.

When we pack to leave, we turn back to the window overlooking the old Neosho riverbed. Without saying a word, my husband moves the ghost-woman's rocking chair back to the original spot. He takes out a cigarette, breaks it open, and leaves tobacco on the window sill, food for spirits. Then we take our leave.

Neosho River Sunrise

The prissy bird tiptoes
wet sand.
Its long piercer-beak sips
river,
spears gnats,
zigzags the dropping
current.

*

Liquid ribbons shatter
at dam's edge and so—

it wades the cusp,
step-steps on sunken rocks
overflow,
unshaken amidst
this roar.

*

A solitary brown topaz
glows against
mink-brown river surface:
plumage gleams
in the muddy Neosho.

Its white underbelly, like foam,
dissolves into froth,
moves into water,
out of water.
    Is lost.

My Grandfather Raises Rabbits

In his exile my Lenape grandfather raised rabbits—
angora, cinnamon, French lop with downturned ears.
Mena-poose—the spirit of rabbits—never came to him
but plenty of furred, fleshy *wa-poose* bred
in backyard cages stacked across the lot.
He dressed them out at ten pounds of meat
then traded for milk, eggs, and pellet feed.

The Depression deepened but rabbits cared
nothing about loss, only the slant of winds
and warmth of littermates. They ate greens
and quietly watched him move about the pen
as he stayed away from his brothers and mother.
In town, he learned to get by on his own.

A Lenape Indian Grandfather's Biography

He farmed his mother's land and left.
He opened a garage and went broke.
He worked at slaughter houses and quit.
In Oakland he worked the docks.

He traveled North and South and East.
He hoboed in Oregon and came back.
He clerked for a drug store and went broke.
He worked on the railroad and got hurt.

He managed a liquor store and stayed.
He smoked, he drank, he gambled
and came up a winner at last —
two of his children lived.

Our Grandfather's Turquoise Ring

West

> My brother asks, Where is
> that old Indian ring Grandfather wore,
> that dark-lake one, the shade
> of haze-creased afternoon skies?

South

> I remember our mother's dresser
> filled with silk embroidery floss
> and a man's heavy ring, streaked
> with dark veins, like his hand.

East

> Once sunrise polished its beauty
> as he crossed a red-brick street.
> Flat horizons doubled over as neatly
> as his monogrammed handkerchief.

North

> He wore it to honor his grandparents.
> He wore it to honor winter snows.
> He wore it to honor cedars and pines.
> He wore it to honor the mountains.

Earth

> As he sat on a bench and smoked
> he saw clouds layering thin sky
> > like seams of Cerrillos blue ore
> > folded into bedrock—copper seams

Sky

> > tempered with winter moonlight
> > and mixed with silver runoff.
> He watched as cloudbanks rolled
> across rooflines and changed to rain.

Center

In the drawer I found Grandfather's ring,
a mirror-bright band set with a cabochon—
a smooth-domed turquoise stone
moving its own measure of years.

Fire and Grass

1.
Jake Bruner, old drover, I see your shadow
flicker among the flames as ranchers
draw fire sticks along withered bluestem.

I see you—my illiterate mystery ancestor,
husband to two Marys—perhaps on horseback,
passing between Kansas and the Territory:

maybe an outlaw, maybe a Flint Hills saint
still tasting fragrance of this spring day
and the sweet *kinnikinnick* smell of leaves

rising to heaven, releasing winter spirits
into wind and skies of red-tailed hawks.
Mosaics of fire and ash hide your soft bones

yet I carry your skeleton's thick pattern
and also your blood. Together we see fire
erupt before us and feel the cleansing heat.

2. Chiaroscuro
Most eerie: the sight of moonlight on charred pastures.
Inky black shadows rise against snow furrows.

Against far ridges a snake writhes in yellow.
Burnt flecks and snow mix through pearly firelight.

And behind the horizon: black angus cattle sleep
with burly bison and hidden glacial mountains.

I saw this twenty years ago and have never forgotten
fire and snow, fire and the unnatural burning moon.

3.
At evening the wind dies down
and damp soil grows clammy.
Flames lick the edge of roads
and the black hems between.
Thistles and cedars shrivel.

Once fires burned creek to creek
but now they outline fence posts
and asphalt. Their perfume
blows east to bare towns where
radios murmur through streets

but here blue racers excite the grass.
Ground squirrels hunker
in a cosmos where stars
turn into cinders, collapse
and sift into galaxies of fire.

4.
The valley is a pipe bowl.
The wind is its breath.

Dried grass is kindling.
Fire scorches like summer sun.

My mother lies buried here
and also my father.

My children were born here
and grew like bluestem.

Smoke is my prayer
rising beyond stars.

> *Release me, release me*
> *Release me, release me*

Columbarium Garden

"Nothing would give up life:
Even the dirt kept breathing a small breath." Theodore Roethke

Cold sun brings this mourning season to an end—
one year since my mother's death. Last winter thaw
my brother shoveled clay-dirt, she called it gumbo,
over what the crematorium sent back. Not her,

but fine powdery substance, lightened, all else
rendered into invisible elements. That handful
of a pouch, un-boxed, was tucked into plotted soil,
the churchyard columbarium, a brass plaque the last

permanence, and the brick retaining wall. Finally
my mother is a garden, day lilies and chrysanthemums
feeding from that slight, dampened, decomposing ash.
Her voice stilled. One ruddy robin in the grass, dipping.

Moraine Shadows Landscape

The Glow-worme showes the Matine to be neere, And gins to
pale his uneffectuall Fire: Adue, adue, Hamlet: remember me."

Spirits of the dead rustle
in my left ear. *Remember me.*
Remember me. In half-light
a black owl wings through time
on glider wings. Sunset.
Ghosts become dark's wind
broken by towering ridges
of moraine and stippled stubble.

My dead niece shakes
her veil of black wavy hair
across my face and I smell
her musk, her lost beauty.
My father-in-law brings
another jade necklace
and forgives me.
It is Solstice. Sunset.

In dim illumination
another vision sharpens.
My mother rises and walks.
My grandmother, who outlived
everyone she knew, limps,
sapphire eyes still on fire.
Friends appear, and a child.
Then horizons fold over.

Tree limbs reach heaven,
un-leafed. Black hawks sit high
rearranging feather cloaks.
They follow winter
even to this far frostline.
Any motion snaps their eyes.
In early glow-worm dawn
they harvest fruits of the night.

29

Red-Tailed Hawk: Medicine Bundle

After a Field Museum photograph by Terry Evans

What power remains in this medicine bag
assembled by a hawk: "Crickets and snake
in the stomach pouch," with specks of sage.
Mottled down covers the bundle, as soft

as our own bodies. We make the same magic
with blood and breath of others' lives.
The hawk's tailfeathers are a dance bustle,
stained with ocher-red and night-sky colors.

This reliquary holds ghosts of mice
and windless, winter night full moons.
Its crystalline eyes still pierce clouds
and spiral processions of light.

Deer Season

In an unmown yard of dry grass, I miss
the deer themselves, but instead find tamped
outline of their bodies and inhale their faint
aroma. I see that secret bower they create
when they press together all night and breathe.

Moonlight speckles their hides. At sunrise, like stars,
they disappear. But since they are shamans
their spirits remain. Here, presence of deer is tangible,
even as sun brightens. Their scent leaves this haunting.
Bent straw traces fragile glyphs, their stories,
as they step backwards into my memory.

Trailhead

"We were Americans of the middle border where the East was
forgotten and the one great western road no longer crawled
with wagons." Loren Eiseley.

1.
On the Oregon Trail
migrations continue west.
Movement defines stasis.
One solid plane of commitment:
That place defines loss.
I remain and lose the future.

Watch for travelers
who risk what they have
for what might happen.
Children die of snakebite.
Bad water. A blizzard.
Rain gathers and slips away.

2.
What is not seen: the deer behind the hedge.
Half a sky of warblers tucked into grass.
The back side of cumulus clouds.
Rain on the mountains miles west.
Rosettes of unripe sunflowers.

What is not heard: thunder.
The unceasing cheeps of sparrows.
A grasshopper unsettling the grass.
My boot crunching dried fieldrows.
Gusts ruffling the hawthorns.

What is passed:
How my grandfather ran prairies.
How my father watched for red-tails.
How cloud strata arrived at night
just as my first son was born.

32

Two Gates

I look through glass and see a young woman
of twenty, washing dishes, and the window
turns into a painting. She is myself thirty years ago.
She holds the same blue bowls and brass teapot
I still own. I see her outline against lamplight;
she knows only her side of the pane. The porch
where I stand is empty. Sunlight fades. I hear
water run in the sink as she lowers her head,
blind to the future. She does not imagine I exist.

I step forward for a better look and she dissolves
into lumber and paint. A gate I passed through
to the next life loses shape. Once more I stand
squared into the present, among maple trees
and scissor-tailed birds, in a garden, almost
a mother to that faint, distant woman.

Delaware Guardian Doll

"Sometime during the long middle years of wandering,
the four-plus decades in Missouri and Kansas, Grandma ...
became keeper of the Ohtas, the Delaware dolls."
Lynette Perry, *Keeper of the Delaware Dolls*

Delaware Dance Doll:
    black hair bound in a bun
red-painted oak face
    ruffled, brooched collar
maroon skirt, flounced
    oak leaf appliqué
beaded, cuffed moccasins
    two-hundred years gone

and Great-Grandmother is here
        buried by the North River
        in Wyandotte Cemetery
        with her Dolls.

I remember my mother's stories:
    They rode city trolleys to buy dolls
        store-boughten raggedy anns
        and porcelain English ladies.
    At home they made cornhusk women
        and carved wooden Madonnas.
    She taught me to belt a hollyhock bloom
        and shape the red-petal skirt.

And still my mother keeps dolls
    with sets of clothes resewn each year:
        girls in tiered skirts, boys in black vests
        blonde and black-haired, brown eyes and blue
        miniature leather shoes reaching down.

Another Custer Story

This one is true. I am in the family cemetery leaving tobacco for Grandfather and purple daisies for Grandmother. It's hot summer, over a hundred degrees. Inside the fence, an old man is mowing the grass.

He stops and asks who are my people? and I say the Roots and Bairs, out of Ohio, the Killbuck River area. "Roots are in the other section," he says. "Were they Indian? Root sounds Indian." I look at him again, at his small blue eyes and hooked nose. He has a friendly and ancient face, with wrinkles that don't come until ninety. I say, yes, Delaware and Mohegan. I ask about my cousins, and he knows all of them and their news. His name is Stevens but it's changed from something French.

And then he says "George Armstrong Custer was my grandfather Nevin's brother." I don't know what to say. All his great-uncles—George, Tom, and Boston Custer—died ingloriously at the Little Big Horn.

In my silence, he continues, "They were from Ohio, two counties from your folks. Their grandmother was Shawnee tribe." And so another twist for the stories: the best-known Indian fighter was Indian.

Circles of Grass

In this field I hear the silence that remains after mourners leave a grave—pause, caesura, absence of wind. What remains is a leafy archive spiraling around my feet.

The history of a site is its weathering. This is my mother's funeral fire, after the guests depart. This is debris from last winter's snow. After abandonment, this remains as a cold hearth. Winter birds left, and summer birds have not yet arrived.

I enter another door. Transition from one place to another: this continues indefinitely.

On limestone bluffs, a painter inscribes spirals, crosses, hands, and stars. As soon as I assign meanings, they change.

Seven Marriage Offerings

For Pamela and Michael Tambornino

Ani Sagonige, Offering to the North
    Blue skies, clarity, purity of cold wind:
    After the winter cleansing we see pines.
    Each needle is crisp. This clarity we need.

Ani Dalohnige, Offering to the West
    The ripe harvest of setting sun, its yellows:
    Each evening as we reflect, in tandem,
    we share the day's stories, then rest.

Ani Gvnage, Offering to the South
    Southern sun heats emotions:
    some days too impetuous. In black night,
    and in all conflict, we learn compassion.

Ani Wodige, Offering to the East
    Each morning, without gall, we see a new sun:
    Each dawn we are newlyweds, humbled
    by the brown river and its red mists.

Galvladi, Offering to the World Above
    The heavens rise beyond our sight,
    past the sun, moon, planets and stars:
    We accept power beyond our senses.

Eladi, Offering to the World Below
    Beneath us lie the remains of all beings
    and the kingdom of rocks and finally
    the fire of this planet's hearth: our home.

Offering to the Center
    Heartbeats repeat within us again and again,
    our own fires, winds, stony bones, muddy flesh:
    On this day, two hearts measure one breath.

Anniversary

One perfect mallard
doubling itself
in afternoon reflection

two curved heads dabbling
reappearing, disappearing
into water-bowl lake:

slide and blur
until just the tails
touch, tip, shatter,

Dear, like us
two images folded
into a single pose

slipped into dark
earth's rest
held only by breath

until to awaken
to kiss and uncover
two touching, touched skins.

Menominee Rez, Sunday Morning

Church bells ring and rez dogs
sing tenor. We cross St. Joseph's
back to the forest, past two boys
rolling toy trucks in a yard.
Peals and wolf howls rise
amid drifting pine smoke.

At the logging road we find
a buffalo-nickel key ring
and Marine Corps tags.
Ripe cattails outline a dry pond
where seven clans gathered
years before French Sundays.

Last night, stars streaked
the black void but now blue
spreads thin like a Great Lake
misplaced in the sky.
Sun burns through pine needles,
piercing all our eyes.

Reds

for David Low

Merlot

> So easy to sip with friends
> on a eucalyptus hillside
> no one can see from the road.

Malbec

> A flamenco dancer's boot
> taps staccato on the floorboards
> a continent away. I follow the beat.

Cabernet Sauvignon

> On a Parisian street corner
> the chef leans on brick and smokes.
> He inhales muddy river mist.

Shiraz

> My grandmother's perfume bottles
> reek of crystalline jasmine.
> Sun bounces through their facets.

Zinfandel

> Stewed raisins spill
> through a layered late sky.
> Carols arise across the street.

Chianti

> A fire truck alarms the neighborhood.
> After-images will stain the breeze
> all next week.

Pinot Noir

> Bedrock seines rain and roots.
> Volcanoes dissolve. Old seas melt.
> The last pool is a liquid mirror.

Sangiovese

> Better than the taste of honey
> is this ancient wound.
> Old gods bleed beneath the vineyard.

Osage Beach, Lake of the Ozarks

For Tom

1.
Time collapses as we walk mountains
and find hand-worked chert edges
among the jumble of wrecked boulders.
Form shatters into edges, reforms into use,
falls away again into broken bird points.
The afternoon stretches into a labyrinth:

which path around that scrub oak?
What turns before we leave each other?
A new moment arises among geodes
at our feet—crystals folded into matrix.
We find surprise caught in our hands,
like a rockslide seized against slope,
like stone eroding into sandy grasslands
where fits—the soft wet print of a panther.

2.
Chert—alabaster white, luminous
against dirt, blocky chunks, and blades
scattered, accidentals among tree roots:
we walk among knives, step carefully
as we speak, breathe with the mountains
as they rise and fall, old *Aux-Arcs*.

Some veins of the stone giant run red
as our own blood, ferrous seams
broken from rock spine underfoot,
rosy as the soft damp of your mouth.
We are rouged by the same mother
as this expanse of Cambrian boulders.
These few lavender flints fell from stars
millennia ago, into these colorless waters.

3

The steps lead eastward and downward
from the young Colorado mountain range,
to spread of silty plains among foothills,
into oak savannahs and coal beds, deeper,
farther back into the worlds before this one
with simpler life forms—mussels—

then silence in the stone tombs underfoot.
We walk through catacombs of time
this spring afternoon, near each other,
far from each other, small streambeds
for trails, no wind but then some crows,
deer tracks, and a distant panther chokes.
On the hike up rocks this could be the day
we first met. Or a day nothing happened.

4.

In river country, flint nodules rest
among limestone sea bottoms, unexplained,
glassy among the porous tangle of shells
and ferns and crinoids. Spring storms unearth
campsites laid over ancient wreckage,
fresh water washing over dried-out depths

and thousand-year-old tools. We stop
as two geese part the clouds and murmur.
Below, we find a woman's hide scraper,
bone-white, hand-sized, and decide whether
to leave it to the rain or carry it farther
into this world. Far from mountains
we move more slowly, see horizons.
We turn to the sky for tides and lights.

Cherokee Lessons

I learn the word for bullfrog, *kanuna,*
and remember when we ate frog legs—
kanuna gvtsatlvnv: white meat tender
in batter. *Kanuna a-gwa-du-li.*

Godvnv, crawdads, creep edges
of river shallows, skittering deeper
as I reach. *Godvnv a-na-i.*

Opossums are smiling pigs
under the porch, *siqua utsetsas'di.*
Fairy tales omit these snouted beasts
yet here they lumber through the yard
startling the dogs, teeth protruding.

Sali, persimmons, grow nearby.
I learn how *siqua utsetsas'di* climb
their branches to feast. Hunters shake
them to the ground and kick them.

I watch *saloli,* squirrels. *Saloli a-na-i.*
They chatter and quarrel all day.

My mother hates the mulberry tree,
guwa, because grackles gorge
and drop purple smears on laundry.
I eat its seeded sweetness and know
this summer cosmos has words.

.

Summer Love

Dusk. After love
we walk a teetering balance
of summer twilight.

A tiny
dull-lemon warbler
silhouetted atop a pole

wheezes a melody—
tiny fluff
against sky

blowing wind
into a pipe organ
of passion.

Fragile bones carry
ligaments and musculature,
nearly transparent

yet throbbing whistles
pour through night air,
touching our innermost ears—

almost another lover
moving within, almost
sweet blood warming again.

Elk Medicine

That male elk across the creek
wooed the dozen females
and made their calves.
They sprawl the meadow.
He looks, lowers his antlers,
grazes another mouthful.
Then looks again.

By afternoon the last cow
goes to ground. Rests maybe
while the herd drifts to water.
She stays as they wade the stream.
Finally, sun lower, she rises
with a damp, unsteady child—
his powerful medicine.

On Thompson River

We make love at dawn with
tumbling water
our witness. Then awaken again.

The river speaks differently.
Lisps.
No, falters and restarts.

Magpies out of sight
roughen
their throats against air

like us. We learn this
new talk
how to speak wet syllables

with torrents of breath. How
to touch
and breathe whirlpools.

We learn intricate structures
of waterfalls
how rapids assemble and collapse.

How breath hesitates, moves again
and returns
like a current caught.

Conception

Two identical doves squat
in the pine, plump squabs.

One feeds a morsel to the other,
foreplay before fluttery mount.

Then they regain composure.
Smooth their silken vestments.

Nightfall they roost side by side.
In dawn glow they doze.

Within pale fluff one of them
holds a tiny cup of yolk.

Like once I was held.
And you.

Inside Her Belly: The Spine

This creation story begins with fog.
Oceans are the sky. Valleys are dark voids.

The hero has delicate fish bones
connected to a lumpen head.

Or delicate fern-leaf vertebra
curl around uncertain middle continents.

Or is this a water snake's spine,
or a limestone fossil's—returning to life?

II.

Walt Whitman
and the Cheyenne Prisoners of War
Lawrence, September 15, 1879

He wears a flowing, open-necked shirt
and like Cheyenne men, he wears long hair.
He carefully bird-walks with a cane,
maybe faint from the heat or his illness.

The stone jailhouse is unexpectedly stuffy
so they sit outside for the breeze.

Whitman will write how they ignore the mayor—
"big gun of officialism" he calls him—
but the Cheyenne greet *him* and shake his hand.
Wild Hog is the orator, and Old Man is counselor.

*

The men sign their story:
How they watched fifty children die of measles.
For months they had no meat.
They broke out from Fort Robinson in deep snow.
The men were all shot except these few.
They wait for months and become celebrities.
Reporters bring tobacco for interviews.
They go to a circus and see an elephant.
They talk to senators and now this white-bearded man.

*

Whitman does not understand their precise gestures
but he remembers his Indian Affairs job
and how he visited Cheyenne Indians at their hotel:
"I had the good luck to be invariably receiv'd
and treated by all of them in their most cordial manner."
Whitman writes how they "know the difference"
about him, apart from words. Whitman will describe
"that topography of your western central world—
that vast Something, stretching out."

*

For court the wives and daughters arrive,
the girls modest in red shawls.
A reporter writes of their beauty.
They sit outside the jail, pray, and smoke.

The judge will give his verdict: not guilty.
The men will return North to the homeland
and renew their hold on existence:
    Wild Hog, Old Man, Blacksmith, Tangled Hair,
    Left Hand, Porcupine, Crow.

Emory Honoway (*Whitman, An Interpretation in Narrative*, Alfred A. Knopf, New York and London, 1926) documents Whitman's meeting with Cheyenne prisoners.

Custer's Sleigh
at the Ft. Leavenworth Museum

Untouched, Libby's baby-pink
wooden sleigh is still adrift
in Leavenworth County hills—
lacquered wood still bright,
and long saber-curved runners.

It was she who ordered
the carpentry, who instructed
the German woodworker
to assemble two benches
and the sweep of headrest.

She made the best of idleness,
rumors and postponements,
her letters lost—or delivered
and ignored. The sleigh could return
his attention to their matrimony.

She approved the snow carriage
and engraved bronze plate:
"Made for General Custer
by William Keiser, 1872"
and awaited the infrequent news.

Pontiac Hall Ghost

At the crossroads of Pontiac Hall lives a ghost.
He leans on the old cedar tree, fading against it.
The shredded bark drapes loosely around the tree
like an ill fitting Halloween costume.

At nightfall the ghost emerges and smokes.
Sometimes students see him and run.
Even during drought his corner remains dark.

One sunny day I followed painted stripes
across the intersection. I thought about
my husband's warm arm around me.
I startled and dodged a Chevy van.

I keep walking past that old cedar tree,
and I am still here to tell you about it.

Geronimo's Boots Leave Town

An argument for NAGPRA

I hear Geronimo's boots left town
and his wife's and daughter's boots
went with them—a family of shoes.

They lived silently in an artist's
basement collection for years
safe except for one flood.

Now they are for sale. The label says:
"Geronimo bought cowboy boots
and threw away these moccasins—

fringed deer skin, knee-high.
Chiricahua. 1886." In such leather
the desert trickster made stories:

> *The time he slipped off a mountain*
> *when surrounded by the army*
>
> *The time he shapeshifted*
> *so another man's face appeared*
>
> *The time he cut off one wife's nose*
> *for fooling around.*

He had medicine that made him invisible
but when they thought he was gone
he returned with a wife and watermelons.

For his final trick he pretended
to lose his mind, the price
for all that power, but instead

he was practicing how to stay alive
in all kinds of skins—first buckskin
and now domesticated cowhide.

William Allen White House

It was afternoon when my long-dead father
drove us across town to Red Rocks
on Exchange Street. It had a mausoleum air

until we entered through the kitchen door.
William Lindsay greeted us. I do not remember
conversation, but I saw walls of books,

high ceilings, and Italian leather chairs.
The men were gruff bears in summer coats
with forest paneling around them. Newspapers

lay about and a girl's portrait, caught in mirrors.
I remembered how Mary White fell from a horse
and died, at my young age. I felt mortal fears

in the framed elegy. I avoided shadowy corners
and studied the armoire with Anastasia's plates.
Father, W.L. and the house—all were half lit.

Soon after both men died and left me with memories
of carved tusks, distant and broken conversation,
and how Catherine the Great's ruby goblet glimmered.

I Still See the Ghost of Langston Hughes

After forty years, he meets me every day.
Sometimes he takes the pen from my hand
and starts a line, then changes into a boy
pirouetting fancy steps down Vermont Street.

This is Langston's heaven. He travels easily
from Cuba to Harlem and all his hometowns.
He visits his brother's grave in Joplin.
In Lawrence he whispers to all the poets.

Downtown I hear blues musicians
like Lee McBee shout country sorrows
or hear the Bopaphonics sort Langston's lines
into endless hip-hop rounds of rhymes.

On the library steps where he walked
I hold books with ivory, porous pages.
Sometimes I sense a boy's breathing
lost in a travel novel or New York drama.

I drive by his junior high school and recall
his victory over a prejudiced teacher.
I go to movies in the same opera house
where he saw silent films and vaudeville.

In autumn I hear football fans roar
a few blocks from his grandmother's house.
The sharp wind rises, awakening dry oaks.
Then I hear his restless, restless feet—ready to go.

For John Moritz, One Morning (1946-2007)

Pointillist geese on a translucent pond turn us
    backwards in time, that mirror
reflection of now, but askew—

to a roadside we knew, half-frozen.
    Those many geese hang, *perdido*,
on open water as ice edges sharpens.

Down the bank, a frozen dog hunkers
    encrusted in storm's white breath.
Morning's sun-daggers flashes through—

and today, less one soul, light still skims
    this glacial valley, and an icy telephone wire
where listens: an iridescent line of starlings.

I Miss You, Sonny Kenner

A year dead and still
I miss those china-blue eyes
set in that wise master face
those stories about Bird
and growing up Black and poor
and memorizing poetry
for sustenance.

I miss those all-night dances
and his band easing along
experienced like old lovers
knowing just what touch
to electrify our blood
as Mustang Sally rides
the sunny side of the street.

I miss the sermons
set in amongst the tunes
like rubies in silver
about gratitude and about family
with the bass line underneath
so it all seems solid.

I miss the stories
about where bebop started
about old Kansas City
and singers who shouted
and Minnie the Mooch
and all those music men
who held up Count Basie
and traveled long roads

but he came home
to compose parables,
to let kids sit in with his band
to learn those lyrics
phrased just so right.
So natural he should be
part of this world.
He cannot be gone.

Ark City Run

My father drives a train
hundreds of miles, alone in the engine,
and returns, the same miles.

At home he never speaks
of the double life, double speed
away from us, always outbound

until as an old man, he softens.
He limps to the ladder, climbs
aboard, settles on a seatpad

and hurtles into night,
the locomotive shuddering apart
his eardrums and backbone cartilage.

At rest he tells me of pain,
of fused vertebra, neck almost frozen,
but on his travels he watches birds:

each trip, hawks and larks,
herons and egrets—
along river wetlands and in fields,

their vivid wild lives
spread across landscapes, empty
except for their winged shapes.

Each loop, his railroad "runs,"
counting down to the last,
he peers out train portals.

He carries binoculars and studies
bird books. The hawks he loves
best—russet-red, white-bellied:

summer hawks circling,
suspended for hours
then diving for garter snakes

or winter sentinels on poles,
solitary hunters posted
against northern snows.

He died in this season,
as the Arkansas River froze
and red-tailed hawks sat silent.

He was not unhappy to go.
Life under a wide sky
gives no illusion of permanence.

Bare trees formed scaffolds
against clouds. Hawks hunched
in them like fists.

Elegy for Autumn

1.

Caught like a finch in the apple tree's crossed arms,
my father's face appears, a pale image in a maze,
and I remember his lopsided, stroke-stricken face
and his blue-coal eyes alive within immobile flesh.

Then I look again at tangled bare tree limbs.
The finch reappears, red-tipped, dark against wood.
Wind gusts strongly until bark breaks free and flies.

2.

What I want to recapture is
walking through papery cottonwood leaves—
yellow hearts—and a few crimson stars.
This was the first time I understood autumn
as different from other on-rolling days.

My father was somewhere else, lost even then,
on the railroad and gone again for weeks.
I loved the basket of red jonathans
he found in the world somewhere
and carried into our cellar to sweeten.

3.

I remember winter dirt, a muddy orange clay,
laid bare after frost and cold rains.
I learned how dust drops out of clouds and settles.

I remember my father's breathing across the hall,
across unmapped darkness of walls. How he
heaved into metal-springs, and the radio clicked off.

4.
And now in another rest,
his weighty, dense, ashy grit
is boxed and sunken
into the walled churchyard.

I am left to long grief
for something neither of us understood
or expected from each other—
how our love did and did not fail.

Faith

The ensemble of geese overhead
strains, forthright, necks stretched
into the sun. They are black motes
showing no doubts, paddling wind,
outracing a sleety bank of night.

III.

Buried City

1.
Spiro Mounds. A buzzard
slides edgewise into clouds
and then returns to view.

We read the guidebook:
"Imagine a living city
with children and running dogs."

But around us: silence.
The plaza is a broken surface
empty of ball players.

A warbler churs wind
while off the trail
we leave tobacco offerings.

On top of mole dirt diggings
appears an obsidian blade
and a flat black plume:

the living earth raising
dark forms even now
into balance of sky.

2
And over the ridge
tucked into its final roll
lies an armadillo—

its shell patterned,
tiered and sectioned
with lozenges and diamonds.

The animal king lies on a bier
ornamented with armor
and motionless to our eyes

but it moves through grass
slowly into the buried city
hidden from our sight.

3.
What lies below:
    blankets of buffalo yarn
    Mexican parrot feathers
    capes of turkey plumes
    maize and sunflower seeds
    tobacco and squash
    "little brother of war" sticks
    chunkey stones
    charcoal smell of cookfires
    echoes of clackers
    low voices and lullabies
    a child's first breath.

A Mound Builder's Geography

Wyandotte County

The Shawnee prophet *Tenskwatawa* lies buried at White
Feather Spring, a Kansas City creek. His difficult name,
"Open Door," is not memorialized in the city's place names.
It refers to his prophecy, as he had access to the other
world. But some histories renew each time we speak:
"Osage" Street. "Wyandotte" County. "Missouri" River.

The river highway follows bluffs along the second
terrace, just above floodwaters. Here would be the place of
homesites, facing east, to feel the rising sun's first touch.

These bluffs resemble those of Walking Bear Mound at
Prairie Du Chien, along the Mississippi, but in southern
regions, no such animal mounds rise. Along the Missouri
River banks are geometrical mounds. These Hopewell
barrows fit within curves of the grassy upper banks, so
small that they blend in with cottonwoods. As signs in the
landscape, they barely suggest people passing through this
river corridor.

Douglas County

Nearby, a friend's land contains a large burial mound.
When the family bought the land, they were told the knoll
on the eastern boundary was a Native site. No other
information came with the land, except knowledge this had
been home to Kaw Nation people. The family decided never
to disturb the mound, and it remains untouched, hidden
under a cloak of cedar. Kaw people still claim it and visit.

Such mounds are often on high ground, with pleasing
views of the surrounding landscape. Coyotes, foxes, wild
turkeys, and deer still cross the game trails. To the
northwest, a notch in the horizon holds the sun on the
shortest day of the year. Another gap marks the
southwestern range of the summer sun. At night, shadows

fall across the Ice Age lakebed that forms the valley. All these views spread around the mound.

Another mound, much smaller, is in southern Douglas County. My husband and I hiked these wooded hills and small creek several times. Once we found a vandalized limestone slab burial. At first we did not discern the nearby mound settled against a creek bank, facing the morning sun. It was built into the side of a river, almost indistinguishable from the surrounding lumpy, rocky bluffs. It is simply a miniature hill, thirty yards in diameter. No distinctive markings are visible, and so it continues.

St. Louis

Sixty-eight mounds remain of Cahokia, an old city on the Mississippi River. Plowed fields and a trailer court cover the northern edge of the original grounds, and some mounds are mere swellings. Others are building foundations, and some are burials. Some align with stars and sun. Next to one, on the westernmost edge, cedar poles formed a Stonehenge calendar circle.

The largest, Monk's Mound, is designed like step pyramids of Mexico, but made of packed dirt instead of stone. It dominates the city. Around the central plaza, mounds are situated along the four spiritual directions, so the layout creates a landscape of theology.

Once, when riverways were the easiest routes, this site and Spiro Mound were trade centers of the continent. Cahokia's creek is a road to the Mississippi, which leads to the Gulf and beyond. This city of quiet, grassed-over roadways would be the largest ghost town on the continent.

Four Gifts from My Grandfather

Cedar

	grayhair	evergreen	bristle
	pungent	brittle	specter

Seed

	wild rice	amaranth	corn
	river silt	headwater	star

Sand

	silicate	slick	quartz
	particles	glisten	ripples

Salt

	shine	crystal	prism
	blood	seawater	sting

Downy Woodpeckers

Velvet raccoon-mask
over eyes and cheekbones.

    Winter dancer in scarlet taffeta.

Black-and-white cloak
with skullcap of red.

    A stranger in town, snowflakes caught in his hair.

White-vested breast.
Scallop-stippled wings.

    Ice skater, red muffler flying.

Long tailfeathers
with ladder-back steps.

    Winter shaman under a black-beaded robe.

Cloud Break / Looking East

"Thus walking—as art—provided an ideal means for
me to explore relationships between time, distance,
geography and measurement." Richard Long

The plowed field and gravel road are sculptural,
just as glacial scourings of valleys reorder
the first landscape. Eroded mountains
underlie this day's rouge sun. Panorama
reduces to this moment.

Loose earth resettles into wreckage
of spring-flooded creeks. An artist standing
in afternoon shadows also stirs a new world.
He is like Buzzard of Cherokee people—
the being who flew over Appalachia,
his wings dredging the valleys.

The painter, alone, outside a walled studio,
paces his designs on the land. He uncovers:
"time, distance, geography, measure."

Next to the Garden Globe

The birdbath's rotten concrete edges
feel granular. Sand peppers the cracks.
In the bowl: a drink of wet decay.
Wind frets the oaks.

I am a child again
stolen into the neighbor's garden.
Fluff from a white-breasted bird
spirals on murky surface.

Below: darker reflection—
the future, indefinite, alongside
my rippling hand. Water's face
falsely shapes a circle.

Its green eye mirrors—
      a sampling of cumulous
      the backyard juncos
      corner of an old woman's house.

Portraiture: Grandmother Carrie

My grandmother loved beautiful things: Chinese cloisonné, art deco silver bowls, dinner rings, poetry of T'Ang Dynasty poets, Puccini's operas, and elderblow. She loved the trance of artifice. She had an elegant house with fine silverware and a servant. All this was lost before I was born.

She loved flowers. She taught me flower arranging, *ikebana*. She grew up in a household of sisters who embroidered, sang, and sketched. All her life, my grandmother tried to recreate that family. I was a stand-in for Ruby or Eileen or Annie. I imagined myself a pretty girl in lace.

She hung paintings around her last living room: a violin and Van Gogh's sunflowers. She listened to opera on the radio and wept.

She took me to the window to see elderberry on tall stems. She watched the butterfly migration through fields of milkweed. For a friend's wedding anniversary, she found twenty-five four-leafed clovers. Her eyes were the color of rain.

Water Rising: New Orleans That Monday

The waitress filled my glass with tapwater.
I saw clear blue cubes and panes of light.

As I swallowed, my friend's phone buzzed.
When I glanced up, her face had stopped.

 "The water has started to rise," she said.
Then eerie silence stretched between us.

> Far away mouths fill with mud. Land turns inside out.
> A fetid surge pries away a man's fingers.

> An old woman goes under. A child.
> A man chops a hole in his attic.

As people die, I hold a sunlit globe of water.
I set down the glass, but I never leave that table.

Cormorants at Clinton Lake

How we struggle to keep fleshed
these bodies we are born to—
plumed or bare-skinned:

like shadows among waves
shifting positions while winds raise
watery mazes across the lake.

Dark fowl flocks may emerge,
seated, their legs hidden below.
Periscoped necks are hooks.

They may dive long moments,
rise, gasp sleety air, rare back,
and refit this incessant puzzle.

At last they lift into fog.
Twilight silent, they oar slow beats
through veiled cloud banks.

Out of sight but still present
they take breaths, fly, breathe,
and bleat to us across distance.

Great Plains Geology

for Joan Nothern

Buteo hawks track the zoomed-out map:
glyphs on a blue scroll,
moving Roman numerals.

I walk furrows and see a Swainson's hawk
erect as a post. It rises from stubble,
glides, and dips for the kill.

The distant river treeline traces
a jigsaw fitting of Ice Age erosion.
Sun dims, slides, finally buries itself here.

Flint Hills Grasslands

for Daniel Low

Our eyes travel into blue haze
forty miles and more. I tell my son
about our several-great grandparents
who lived just west of this summit.
Their graves lie in a cedar grove,
In a valley where their voices mixed
into a blur of gusting west winds
like these rushing into our ears.

I tell him about a photograph
of our Delaware grandfather—
his jet hair and deep black eyes
looking at us from a quiet face.
It must have been springtime
because of the flat bluestem
crushed around him in ripples
half a lifetime before his marriage.

I tell my son about Grandmother,
mostly Irish and German,
and lots of questions about her past
but she was born in Kansas
and now lies in the quilt layers
of hills around us, next to him
and next to twin baby girls.

Under the stalled sun
Afternoon seems to hang unmoving,
the solar fire just past zenith,
the clouds heaped to the heavens
above flint-sharp edges of sky.

Red Canyons

Across the ceiling of this land
vultures tilt and coast—
dark eclipses over rocks.

Eighty more miles. A truck passes.
He waves across bloody asphalt.
Then a tableau of feeding starlings.

The next curve, forty buzzards
appear on barbed fence wire
all pink wattles and grins.

And on it goes: past roosts,
past highways, past hearths,
past a road ending at a washout

and disappearing into an arroyo
where the world re-folds into itself.
Red boulders are the last evidence.

Wakarusa Wetlands Prayer

All silence until
I walk by and then—
dried leaves
    take wing.

*

Brown earth stars
visible by daylight

feather explosions
in wind

reassemblings
in pine splays

murmurs simple as air
as sunrise every day.

*

I bluster a swath
through a confused flock.

To the horizon
they line a walkway,

rise, then fall back
exactly in place.

*

Tokens
of common moments

Alice Walker's "everyday use"
small totems

like who I am:
everyday plain

dark blonde or light brunette
markings unremarkable.

Liminal, the quiet one
at table.

Golden Triangle Ghosts

We visit a haunted hotel
at midday, up a steep dirt road.

We enter the lobby, with sunlight
visible on teak and green tiles

but some vital part of the air seems
missing. Our breath quickens.

The wooden filigree will not hold still
in my eyes. A friend whispers

> *The Khmer bas-reliefs on the wall*
> *come to life at night.*
>
> *Tortured soldiers rise from the wood*
> *and limp about the verandah.*
>
> *Even in daylight the servants hear sounds,*
> *moans and unintelligible words.*
>
> *Villagers quit after a few days work.*
> *Only tourists will stay overnight.*

BIA Mementos

For Pemecewan

She tells me:
>At the gun show booths something Indian
>catches her eye, a BIA logo
>in the swirl of gun powder smells.
>
>The man shows her the inscription
>"Wyoming Territory" in raised brass,
>dated just after the Civil War,
>
>and the stamped black number.
>"Do you know what this is?" he asks
>after she pays. "It's a corpse tag."
>
>On E-Bay she finds more for sale:
>"Nice gifts for Christmas" say the pop-ups
>and she sees how Indian wars continue.

There is another count
in Sweetwater, Wyoming:

>"September, Anderson killed near Miners Delight."
>"May, the Lieutenant killed on Big Beaver."
>"August, George Colt killed on North Fork."

From "Indians in Sweetwater County," transcribed by Herman C. Nickerson in *Scrapbook of the South Pass Area.*

Where My Father Went after He Died

Sister calls after the strained funeral
and asks where Father went. She dreamed

and dreamed how he was sorrowful,
lost in a murky formless dark.

His displeased voice resounded
the morose King Lear tone he always had.

She asks me about the urn, the final
placement, perhaps on the mantle?

I call our mother whose mind
wanders dimensions I cannot fathom.

She remembers the funeral home delivery—
maybe or maybe not. She forgets.

Sister calls again. More night visitations.
More raging, weeping, storming.

I call the funeral home director
and indeed the heavy cardboard box

is forgotten, set on a shelf with others
in the front coat closet, abandoned.

Our father is dusty and displeased.
I go pick him up. Sister's dreams stop.

Somehow in that after-place, he learns
how to summon this world for help.

Fourth of July Parade

Southern wind blows the striate flag.
      It is one wing beating.
      No—a beating starry heart.
I pick a clear marble from the sidewalk
      for luck. The nearby river is old.
A dragonfly floats on iridescent blue wings
      far from cat's-eye water shimmer.
Another horse trailer rattles the road.
      The rodeo starts at seven.
The cowboy has a handlebar mustache.
      His wife wears a fringed vest.
Bricks stagger row by row
      down the long aisle of Main.

Exhibition Box of Meadowlarks

After a photograph by Terry Evans
"Drawer of Eastern Meadowlarks"

An invention:
thirty meadowlarks
laid end to end.
Paper seines light
and silver tincture
silhouettes.

*

Meridian sun
still ripens
feathered bodies
but I cannot see
eyes long sealed
or feel how hot
the feather touch.

*

I return forty years later
and listen to
old stars pivot:

those midday-yellow birds
enmeshed
in six-foot bluestem

Flint Hills sparrows
unremarkable

to a solitary child
I once resembled

*

And the constant sky:
those thirty quick heartbeats
the flutter-breaths
the flow of radiance
into feathers
the breeze of sweet
lost west wind.

*

Beaks lunge upward
arranged evening roosts
on telephone wire

sing an unending aria:

their last long whistle
inhaled, never quite released.

Dreams of Geese

When a friend was dying of breast cancer, she dreamed of geese. At a hospital visit in Kansas City, deep in an urban neighborhood, she looked up and saw Canada geese flying above the building.

At her next doctor's appointment, she again saw them, above the office building. Dreams continued. She and the birds did a minuet, tracing parallel promenades above and below, conscious and unconscious, through the final months of her illness. Sometimes they were in dreams and sometimes actual winging Vees over the hospital. Realities interchanged.

After she realized the *pas de deux* between land movements and air, she sought them out. She visited the nearby lake, to watch their dependable patterns through water and sky. Geese travel easily between wind and water; north and south; spring and fall. Composed in the same loose wedges or alone, they move between life and death.

Flint Hills Twilight

How shadows loosen from sloughs
and rise like floodwater.
Cedars shift rust-green to black.

I cannot tell if I am alone
or maybe with you again
within this diminished light.

*

After another earth-quarter turns away—
this world's quirk of axis—
the sky re-arouses:

     violet and cobalt, then indigo.
        You could be visible
        against the last brilliant sky.

*

Singers and drummers begin the victory song:
this day will not die. Blue enflames the ridgeline,
     a shining serpent twisting and twisting.

     Great space separates each breath.
        I could be on the edge of chasms.
        You could be barely within sight.

*

Before final loss, the moon rises—
orange globe, an exaggerated parallax
of human seasons and repetitions,

as red-tails and voles rest motionless.
You could be in the shadows waiting
or hidden in yesterday's night.

Photography

After a photograph by Terry Evans
"Great blue heron, Texas, 1922"

Its neck recurves
like a ladle handle

It bends into its breast:
a still-life arabesque

*

Stunned flat
in the camera's
extravagant explosion
light is redoubled:

*

 into all herons I can recall:
            specters around the bend
            fog coalescing into wings
            petroglyph tracks in mist

*

and now paper edges
        squared sight of a heron
        frozen. Also borders are:
        my eyes as I multiply

"Trumpeter Swan": Photograph

"It was a dead swan. Its body lay contorted on the beach like an
abandoned lover." Terry Tempest Williams *(Refuge)*

Like an Egyptian mummy
imprinted with muslin weave,
a bundle of feathers folded
into itself, half concealed
yet revelation of wild form:
it hovers in shadow and lines

as I watch, a safe voyeur,
beyond talons and bludgeon beak
and hisses and puffed charges
at my intrusion. Shrouded
flat, obscured and faceless
its silence is a challenge:

how contorted limbs and neck
create lovely, lifeless elegance.

After a photograph by Terry Evans

Kansas Day, January 25

Long winter nights turtles burrow in mud beds
while we drive blotted icy roads. They rest heavy shells
and sleep. Above them, beavers chink domed lodges
and patrol the waterways. Fishing boats hear their slaps.

And in this season of hard weather we gather,
sheltered by timbers and masonry walls.
We repaint ceilings with star animals and hunters.
We remember *"Ad astra per aspera"* as sun tilts south.

IV.

My Diaspora

Look. I might appear to be one small woman
but I embody a genealogy of opposing soldiers—

the Celtic Pict fighting a Saxon invader,
the Irishman fighting an Ulster unionist.

I use a language of seafaring traders and pirates
where borrowed words shuffle subjects and verbs.

The nights may be *weird,* as specters *weird* me.
Spirits might be *manidoowag* or *anitsas'gili.*

On the Potomac a Virginia Englishman falls to an arrow.
An English laborer marries a Seneca woman Jane.

A Georgian named Chapman goes to a Union prison.
An Ohioan mixed-blood dies on a Confederate boat.

All of these were my grandfathers. None were born here.
I live in *Kansas,* a Siouan word for southern winds.

I study Cherokee. *Tsalagi de-ga-de-lo-qua.*
My names are French and Hebrew and Celtic.

Also my mother-in-law gave me an Algonquin name.
Each dawn the diaspora begins inside my skin.

My father kept his grandfather's flintlock in the closet.
His Texan mother feared it killed her Southern kinfolk.

I remember its dark wood, worn stock, and iron fittings.
I remember my mother's diphthongs and Midlands rrr's.

I was born with straight black hair. It curled and lightened.
In the sun I freckle and tan and sunburn all at once.

Democrats and Republicans, Catholics and Protestants,
traditionalist Delawares and Methodist Cherokees.

I have shallow veins for the North. I have tropical blood.
I fit nowhere completely, everywhere a bit. Never do I rest.

Scenes after the Death of William Burroughs

For Wayne Propst

1.

Burroughs said a spider resided in his bedroom closet, but no one believed him. After the old man died, a renter cleaned out the bedroom and a brown recluse spider—the kind whose bite is worse than rattlesnakes—chomped him. This truth raises paranormal questions:

> Perhaps Bill returned as a spider, during the powerful time after a death when a ghost can influence the living

> Or the spider sensed the renter was not Burroughs, and so spiders can sense identities

> Or the old man manifested a spider from his magical ghostly thoughts

> Or simply Burroughs was right all along: there was a spider in the closet?

2.

After he died, they found all his shamanistic paraphernalia—bundles of bones and feathers. This was not unusual. When Professor Ruhe died in a downtown apartment, his relatives found Australian aboriginal items in a locked cabinet. A nephew recognized which etched stones were dangerous. He disposed of the witchcraft killing tools and sold the less dangerous pieces to a foundation in Virginia. Everyone hopes the renter in Burroughs's house will be careful.

3.

After the funeral, the grieving company drove to St. Louis for interment. The hearse driver was a former lover of Burroughs. All 300 miles to St. Louis, the driver described such variations of erotic love that he accelerated to a hundred miles an hour. The entourage arrived in record time.

4.

At a rest stop near Columbia, the funeral convoy stopped. A van of Dead Heads was in the parking lot, trying to decide which way to go next. One of the Heads was reading a biography of William Burroughs.

He looked at a photograph of Burroughs with a woman friend. As the Dead Head looked up, he saw that exact same woman walk out of the toilets. Realities overlapped. "Excuse me," he said. "Have you seen Burroughs lately?" She pointed to the hearse.

The Dead Heads joined the funeral procession, threw dirt on the casket, went to the dinner, and drank toasts. At the wake, long after everyone was very drunk, the bouncer threw them out for performing heterosexual acts in poor taste.

5.

After burial, the photographer and other mourners lingered. Someone asked which gun Burroughs took with him into the afterworld. Before long, several comrades pulled out their heat. They discussed a final salute, but before they could begin, the photographer, who told me this story, headed for the St. Louis river bluffs.

6.

Next came the problem of what to do with the house. Burroughs lived there almost sixteen years. But who would want a haunted, two-bedroom cottage with a full-basement firing range?

Most of the furnishings went to storage, even the roll-about chair that served as Burroughs's wheelchair. The orgone box in the back yard was left abandoned, overgrown with poison ivy.

In the kitchen, ghosts of cats still wrap themselves around the renter's legs when he cooks. Koi in the ponds disappeared, but bamboo flourishes.

Winter Sunday afternoons, local artists mount one-day, one-man shows of art. Wayne Propst's plastic baby head series works well in the space, as well as his shell-casing artifacts.

7.

Finally, despite some protest that a "wife-killer" and communist should not be celebrated, the Lawrence City Commission voted, unanimously, to name the muddy trickle along his house Burroughs Creek. The city paved its eastern side with concrete and noted his name on a map. His journey to the western lands is complete.

I See a Ghost at Watertower Park

Old neighbor with the black lab
looks more sallow than I remember
as he walks by the picnic table
with the dog panting alongside.

I wave quickly as I pass since
he talks more than I can listen.
He lives alone. Two wives died
and the third left a year ago.

All winter I see him walk the dog.
He thins out, fades, looks
not quite well, even gaunter
but then people age differently.

Early spring I ask the neighbors,
"What's wrong with old Mr. So-and-so?"
This is how I find out and check
the obituaries. He died last July.

Death Mask

When my mother died, scarlet blood
bubbled from her mouth. I didn't expect
blood. They had her on a drug all night to keep
her alive until the doctor's morning rounds.
Then he ordered the last prescription, morphine.
The nurse administered the needle, and in four breaths,
the last one a rasp, she was finally dead except blood
flowed out her unmoving mouth. Without muscle flex,
her face collapsed oddly. Quickly she was a stranger.
The next moment an official handed me the form
to harvest organs. I realized they suspended her
for this. My bereavement was outside procedures.

During mourning the vivid red liquid stays in mind.
I remember Plains Indian ledger drawings
where red-penciling by the mouth means death.
Somehow this is a comfort. For days I recall
the brightly alive fluid flowing unhindered
as if all her life, it waited to be released.
Her face had been trapped, tautly held by muscles
in a sequence of unnatural poses, until death.

Teeth: A Tool Kit

A set of knives: paring, filet, and Chinese cleavers.
An abacus: sixteen uppers, sixteen below.
A chess set: "front teeth, pawns / back teeth, pieces."

A necklace for the mouth: a child's ivory beads.
A speech lesson: fricative front-tooth "th," "d," "t."
A embouchure: for trumpets, bassoons, or conches.

A day at the beach: white clams and two augers.
A museum: artifacts from hominid mothers.
Variations: sharp dog teeth or rounded incisors,
        bone-clean gums or wisdom-filled molars.

A mineral kingdom made of chalks and enamels.
A wet, warm cavern with stalactites and stalagmites.
A constellation with white stars planted in pink firmament.

The quotation is from Victor Contoski's poem "Teeth" (*Broken Treaties*,
1973). He describes Polish prisoners beaten until their teeth came out,
The teeth were used for chess sets.

Cap Gun

I spent hours centering red strips
of explosive circles against the spot
where the hammer fell. I killed
how many playmates, rabbits and dogs?
In my mind the murders were real,
with pointing, cocking, and smoky pop.

Then I was old enough for bullets,
first a twenty-two in the backyard
with a pump stock and dull metal pellets
that hailed into tree trunks and doors.

Then came the shotgun for clay pigeons
with power to knock me back.
When the stock bucked I held on, aimed.
The gods forgive me. I was ready to shoot.

Eureka Springs Winter

Victorian porches teeter over Main Street,
painted courtesans showing their age.

Abandoned mansions with boarded-up histories
stagger a winding path up the hillside.

In our jumbled rooming house
we fasten the door behind us, disrobe,

and ease aching knees into steaming baths.
We soak away the chill of a hallway ghost.

After love we find the door ajar, brass fittings
of the lock worn soft as a woman's skin.

Outdoors the lane is narrow as a church aisle.
Pergolas cover spigots and fountains.

Above us, clusters of hissing, barking vultures
populate their own city of elms.

January, and pots still hold geranium rouge.
From a marble bench we watch nothing.

Carrie/Carry A. Nation™

Six foot in stockings.
Stalwart. She had an air
of moral authority.

The hatchet was a trademark
and her patented name:
    CARRY A. NATION™.

Also she published:
"The Hatchet."
"The Smasher's Mail."

A criminal record:
thirty arrests for
Kansas "Hatchet-nations."

Then souvenir pictures
toy hatchet sales
and finally vaudeville.

Downtown bars still post:
"All Nations welcome
except Carrie."

On her grave they wrote:
"She hath done what she could."
but she said it best:

"I am a bulldog running along
at the feet of Jesus
barking at what He doesn't like."

Tornado Angels

The worst kind of tornado fell
like a bad angel, a whirlwind
too vile for the others that float
amidst sheet lighting and dissolve.

Where the cloud hit a church
Bibles flew into the vacuum,
spun clockwise and scattered
over a trailer court.

TV crews interviewed the man
who rode the cyclone, clumsy
like a cow. He dropped back,
bloodied but cured of smoking.

Search dogs nose through rubble
and find two blessed survivors,
and forty souls forgotten by the gods.
Their prayers failed the storm

or they chose to follow updrafts—
levitation straight to heaven,
to the quiet eye of the storm,
sun-lit, not swirling Hell.

The wall cloud drifts to Texas,
full of fenders and lumber,
the tornado coiled and waiting
ready to work the wind's will.

Underground Wonder Bar, Chicago

1
We go down the trickster-rabbit hole
into an overly-real dream
where people distort and weep

where musicians float
in a haze of smoke and buzz
through hibernation hours

where flawed archangels
grant grand piano riffs
tenor sax squeals, cymbal brushes

but take away love,
years of life, and blessed daylight.

2
But then the biker tenor man
opens his lungs and squeals
and honks and gets dirty and gets clean
and makes that saxophone say words
it never knew before this set.

3
But the night belongs to the piano player Coco,
emaciated boy-man who plays classical-gospel-blues-bop
and lifts his eyes every time he thinks of something new
and his shoulders sway and he smiles to unseen phantoms
and maybe he is strung out or lost in those notes—
I want to feed him, make love to him, read his books
hold onto those mazes of sound he weaves and releases.

4.
End of the first set Smokin' Joe the bass player says
"Oh yeah, this is supposed to be reggae,"
but no one notices. This is stone Chicago blue jazz
with his pulsing heartbeat line underneath rock strata,
under the basement floor and the Great Lake itself
a few blocks away. Nothing else.

5.
While six men sweat their blood into mouthpieces,
into rough fingertips, into tense long arm muscles holding
drumsticks—

> The coke dealer wears an undertaker suit, white face
> and black eyes.

> The woman from Santa Fe looks around for someone
> she knows.

> The drunk football buddies break into cheers.

> Three butterfly women hover near the front door.

> A couple diehards listen to night music from angels.

Chicago jazz musicians are Joe Thomas, bass; Coco Preston, keyboard;
Herb Walker, guitar

How I Disappeared in Paris

The first few words
came easily.
"Bonjour." "Beaucoup."
Then I learned *le métro*
and rode quicksilver
trains underground.

Then plunks of rain ran
until walls lay against
boulevards. I myself drained
into *la Seine* until *le* sun
re-rose. The next *demain*
a barge floated through
a *ciel,* no, a heaven of fog.

Then part of my hand
became a *main.* It shook
l'autre. I looked into
a mirror to see
une new *visage mais*
l'image devant un fantome
and je *n'*return *pas* at all.

Nagarjuna Judy

Not-Judy is not emptiness. She is not form.
Not-Judy is not an integer. It or she or he is not a proof.

Not-Judy is not a cell phone stored number nor chai tea
Judy is not stored chai tea nor 841-7010.

Not-Judy cuts a silhouette around Judy-form.
Judy-form outlines a silhouette around Not-Judy.

Not-Judy does not exclaim with enthusiasm
when Not-Judy hears pure form.

Judy does sing. Not-Judy also sings not.
Not-Judy eyes do not smile as her lips do not smile

and in parallel dimensions, Judy eyes
light up when she smiles a clear-sky smile.

An existent Judy verse is not a nonexistent Judy verse.
A *Nagarjuna* Judy is not a nonexistent *Nagarjuna* Judy.

Attention to grammar is not grammar.
Attention to Judy is not Judy.

Judy is a memory and a reality
and non-Judy is not a memory and not a reality.

Words describe what used to be Judy.
What used to be Judy is not Judy.

Not-Judy has no form.
Judy forms this moment in front of us.

Judy dances and does not dance. Judy speaks.
Judy cocks her head that way she does and listens.

The Haunted Secretaire

1.

The one ghost I saw clearly was an old woman sitting in my old antique rocker. The chair had an ornate floral pattern pressed into the oaken headrest, and the woman was flattened, as though she were part of the design. She seemed more like a residual image rather than a separate being. Perhaps porous wood grain lends itself to soaking up impressions, so she was an afterimage rather than a ghost?

2.

Although I sometimes work late hours in haunted buildings at a former American Indian boarding school, I do not see the ghosts. I do not shake their hands, talk, or watch them fade into the wall. Sometimes the lights go on mysteriously, but I do not see ghost hands on the switches.

3.

When I planned to move my parents' secretary or *secretaire*—an old office piece with shelves, glass windows, and a fold-down writing surface—I did not expect trouble. I remembered the writing desk as a silent background figure from my childhood. My father rescued it from an office during a remodeling. Father moved it to our garage, and there it sat untended for twenty years. It was an ungainly six feet tall. Black paint blistered on the shelves, and underneath weathered paint was another dingy layer of white. One of the doors hung on its hinges. In the darkness, it smelled of oil, dank air, and pulp paperbacks deteriorating around it. It was an aging hulk more than a piece of furniture.

4.

One of my father's friends, Jacques LeClaire Haggard, was an Ojibwa Indian man who also participated in the Mason brotherhood. He brought an oversized book sheathed in black cloth. My father would have nothing of social organizations, and he put the book in the secretary, on a high shelf out of reach since no one but Masons should see it.

I made a ladder of an old chair and a pile of books, climbed, and lifted the book from the top shelf. For hours I read about Hermes and Thoth and other Egyptian mysteries. I read about Rosicrucian societies and Pythagorean mathematics. I replaced the cover carefully as the sun fell below the garage windows, returned the book to the high shelf, and shut the glass door over it. The secretary kept my secret.

5.

The deteriorating cabinet continued to be a fixture in the garage. Every fall my father carried a bushel basket of apples and set it next to the cabinet, and after dinner we children turned on a faint light bulb and groped our way to the apples. The secretary had no other purpose than to stand firmly in the darkness with its collection of jars and forgotten books, behind the apples.

6.

When I was an adult, my parents bought a new house. Movers carried the beat-up secretary to a new garage, a larger one with more windows. My sister-in-law saw the secretary, and hidden under layers of grime she found beautiful walnut grain. After she scraped and sanded, swirls appeared in honey-brunette wood. She cream-waxed the surface and shined the windows. She resurrected a handcrafted *objet,* as unexpected as an alchemical hero arisen from putrefied ashes.

Since it was no longer feral, my father reclaimed it to contain his household bills, genealogy documents, political writings, and leather-bound books. When I cleaned out the secretary after his stroke, I found every check stub, every market transaction, and every financial statement of his, his father's, and his grandfather's.

7.

After his death, I spent a winter of weekends cleaning out the secretary, and the family saga unfolded before me. I found my great-grandmother's bill of sale for her house, after she became a widow in the 1920s. I found her maternal grandfather's 1848 obituary notice from his Mason's group in Sydney, Ohio. I found my father's genealogy research, back to his great-grandfather, another William Dotson from Grayson County, Kentucky, born in 1834, just before the Cherokee Trail of Tears violence made him an orphan. I found photographs of this tall man with cropped black hair and his high-cheekboned, serious wife. The rough shelves smelled of mold and very old dust.

8.

One sunny day movers brought the secretary to my house, and I cleansed it. I wiped fuzzy mold from the lower cupboard. The green dust was the kind that forms on bread, not as thick, but just as pungent. As I rubbed a rag across the surfaces, sunlight played on the wood whorls. I found some of the last objects my father ever touched. One of the drawers still contained a key, although it fit nothing.

The movers reassembled the secretary next to south-facing widows. And then—it fit perfectly, as if it always had been in the house. The secretary looked as though its upper shelves always had caught light filtered through our maple trees.

I spent several hours rubbing furniture polish into the thirsty wood, and as I did so, the basement smell gradually lessened. When I opened the writing surface, ink stains showed where a bottle of India ink spilled in a railroad union office and left a permanent reminder of an old-time fountain pen. I also found cigar-sized burns on the front ledge, next to faint puddle stains where whiskey glasses once were set.

With layers of grime removed, the grain showed its fancy arabesque patterns. In the daylight, I could see how a wood worker elaborated the boards with trident designs, four-petaled flowers, and Corinthian edging. The notches and Doric ornamentation seemed freshly made, just arisen from a carpenter's touch.

I turned on a radio. My father often played his mother's opera recordings, and it seemed important to have sound around the secretary, to put it back into the midst of life.

9.

As I rested in the yard, my husband joined me. "Of course, the secretary is haunted," he said. Chills went up my spine. He continued, "It used to be in an office with lots of people around and some late night parties. It needs music, so put the stereo in there. And it needs lots of light. It's scared."

How often had the secretary come close to being discarded? All the years alone in the dark with mold attacking its surfaces brought it closer to destruction, as well. Yet basic to all life, and maybe all form as well, is a momentum toward continuation. Fear might take many forms.

After a few days, when polish dried and bad smells dissipated, the piece of furniture blended against the wall naturally, like another family member, just moving at a slower pace.

Denise Low, 2007-2009 Kansas Poet Laureate, is a literary editor, publisher, author, speaker, critic, and educator. At Haskell Indian Nations University she teaches literature and creative writing. She has been visiting professor at the University of Richmond and the University of Kansas. She serves on the national board of the Associated Writers and Writing Programs (2008-2012). Her *Words of a Prairie Alchemist* and *To the Stars: Kansas Poets* were recognized as Kansas Notable books by the State Library and Kansas Center for the Book. She has awards and fellowships from the Academy of American Poets, Kansas Arts Commission, Lannan Foundation, The Newberry Library, National Endowment for the Humanities, and Roberts Foundation. She earned a PhD at the University of Kansas and an MFA in Poetry at Wichita State University. Her home is in Lawrence, Kansas, where she lives with her husband Thomas Pecore Weso. Websites are: www.deniselow.com and http://deniselow.blogspot.com.

Praise for Denise Low's Writing

"From near the center of the nation-as-we-know-it, Denise Low nimbly engages the timeless elements of poetry—prosody and policy, palette, place, and pang—with a bracingly clear eye and unobstructed view."

    Merrill Gilfillan, PEN/Martha Albrand Award winner

"Denise Low has a voice informed and shaped by the land. She visits the geographies of her region as readily as she does the different regions of literature...Her words rise from the land as the Flint Hills of Kansas."

    Diane Glancy, author of *Stories of the Driven World*, *Designs of the Light Sky*, and others

"This book [*Spring Geese*] is a delight. Low got to use so many good words in ... diligent pursuit of accuracy. I am going to be learning from this book."

    William Stafford, National Book Award winner

"There is a beautiful solitude in Denise's writing....I think we're all blessed by what she sees and what she hears."

    Terry Tempest Williams, author of *Refuge*

"No one understands better than Denise Low the effect of Midwestern vistas of time and space."

    Robert Dana, former Iowa Poet Laureate

"The energy of Low's voice lovingly complements the subjects it describes; it never intrudes. Denise Low knows her surroundings. She has incorporated her sense of place into a vision of maturity and awe."

    Jo McDougall, author of *Towns Facing Railroads* and *Satisfied with Havoc*

"Low's words, like her heart, are grounded in place but soaring in spirit."

    Thomas Fox Averill, Writer-in-Residence, Washburn University

CPSIA information can be obtained at www.ICGtesting.com
Printed in the USA
267425BV00002B/29/P